RELIGIOUS
INTOLERANCE

BY WIL MARA

INTOLERANCE
AND VIOLENCE
IN SOCIETY

ReferencePoint
Press®

San Diego, CA

For more information, contact:
ReferencePoint Press, Inc.
PO Box 27779
San Diego, CA 92198
www.ReferencePointPress.com

LIBRARY OF CONGRESS CATALOGING-IN-PUBLICATION DATA

Names: Mara, Wil, author.
Title: Religious intolerance / Wil Mara.
Description: San Diego, CA : ReferencePoint Press, Inc., [2020] | Series:
  Intolerance and Violence in Society | Audience: Grades: 9-12. | Includes
  bibliographical references and index.
Identifiers: LCCN 2019003303 (print) | LCCN 2019009675 (ebook) | ISBN
  9781682826928 (ebook) | ISBN 9781682826911 (hardcover)
Subjects: LCSH: Religious tolerance.
Classification: LCC BL99.5 (ebook) | LCC BL99.5 .M37 2019 (print) | DDC
  201/.5--dc23
LC record available at https://lccn.loc.gov/2019003303

CONTENTS

IMPORTANT EVENTS IN THE HISTORY OF
INTOLERANCE AND VIOLENCE

1784
Future president James Madison lays out 15 points as to why individual religious freedoms are critical to the budding United States. He also establishes the foundational ideas that eventually lead to the concept of separation of church and state.

100s–200s CE
Adherents of Christianity, a relatively small religion at the time, are routinely persecuted in Ancient Rome.

| 100s–200s CE | 700s | 1095 | 1784 | 1941–1945 |

700s
Following the Arab-Islamic conquest of numerous Middle Eastern countries, Christians are given second-class status in society.

1941–1945
The Holocaust, under Adolf Hitler's regime in Germany, results in the death of more than 6 million Jews.

1095
Pope Urban II launches the Crusades to drive Muslim influence out of the Holy Land and return it to Christian control.

4

2009
President Barack Obama signs the Matthew Shepard and James Byrd Jr. Hate Crimes Prevention Act, which increases the severity of punishments of violence motivated by religion, race, and/or sexual orientation.

2018
Robert Gregory Bowers kills eleven people and wounds another six during a shooting at the Tree of Life synagogue in Pittsburgh, Pennsylvania.

| 2001 | 2009 | 2014 | 2018 |

2014
Islamic State of Iraq and the Levant (ISIL) kills or enslaves thousands of Yezidis in order to drive them out of their ancestral lands in northern Iraq.

2001
On September 11, nearly 3,000 people are killed as a result of terrorist attacks carried out against the United States by Osama bin Laden's al-Qaeda organization.

2018
China undertakes a massive reeducation program in an attempt to convert hundreds of thousands of Muslims away from their religion.

A MASSACRE IN
PITTSBURGH

On October 27, 2018, a horrific example of religious intolerance occurred in the United States. Just before ten o'clock that morning, forty-six-year-old Robert Gregory Bowers walked into the Tree of Life synagogue located in the Squirrel Hill section of Pittsburgh, Pennsylvania. Squirrel Hill is home to a large concentration of Pittsburgh's Jewish population, and Tree of Life was hosting three separate congregations when Bowers arrived. He was somewhat overweight, with short hair and a face full of beard stubble. He might have passed for any other citizen that day—except for the fact that he was carrying one semiautomatic rifle and three pistols.

Bowers considered himself a white nationalist. This meant he believed that the white race was superior to all others and that people of other ethnicities were inferior or dangerous. Among these dangers, in Bowers's mind, were people of the Jewish faith. Judaism is a religion, but its adherents are sometimes targeted based on race. The religious and ethnic components of being Jewish are closely linked. Many forms of religious hatred are intertwined with ethnic or racial hatred, and anti-Semitism—a hatred of Jewish people—is one example of this.

People who knew Bowers did not believe he had harbored this hatred toward Jewish people all his life. A friend who knew him in the 1990s told a reporter, "He wasn't like that back then, with the hate.

Acts of religious intolerance often include violence. Pittsburgh police responded to the shooting at the Tree of Life synagogue.

He was a happy dude."[1] Another friend, who owned a bakery where Bowers had worked in the 1990s, said, "I don't believe he was that anti-Semitic, because we had a couple of Jewish people working for us."[2] But over the years his feelings toward Jews grew into a loathing so intense that he decided to act on it.

At 9:50 on that October morning, Bowers walked into the Tree of Life building and began firing. Two brothers were standing by the entrance to greet visitors. Bowers killed them both, then heard people on the floor below and went straight to the nearest staircase. Once there, he shot and killed more people, including a doctor who

After the shooting at the Tree of Life synagogue, victims' families left memorials and people in the community held vigils. This is a common response after acts of hatred.

had heard the earlier shots and had come to see if anyone needed medical assistance. Then Bowers returned to the first floor and found a group of worshippers taking part in a Shabbat service. There had been thirteen in the group before the shootings began. Five of them managed to escape after hearing the previous gunfire, but Bowers opened fire on the remaining eight. Seven were killed.

Police arrived at 9:59 and exchanged fire with Bowers outside the synagogue. When Bowers was struck by a bullet, he went up to the third floor to hide. By 10:30, a Special Weapons and Tactics (SWAT) team had arrived on the scene. When they entered the building, they too exchanged gunfire with Bowers. Two SWAT officers were shot, one critically. Finally, at 11:08, realizing he had no other chance to survive, Bowers surrendered and was taken into custody. In total, he had killed eleven people and wounded another six. According to reports filed afterward, Bowers shouted several times to police in an attempt to explain his actions. Bowers said, "I just want to kill Jews."[3]

"I just want to kill Jews."[3]
– *Robert Bowers, perpetrator of the Tree of Life synagogue shooting*

In the aftermath of the horror, thousands of notable figures around the world spoke out against Bowers's acts. Former president Barack Obama said in a tweet, "All of us have to fight the rise of anti-Semitism and hateful rhetoric against those who look, love, or pray differently."[4]

RELIGIOUS INTOLERANCE TODAY

Religious intolerance has been a problem in society for thousands of years. It is driven by fear and ignorance. It can be seen in many forms. It can be something as quiet as a passing remark about religious clothing. At the other end of the spectrum, it can be deadly violence like the shooting at the Tree of Life synagogue. Almost every religion has committed some form of intolerance in its past. But religions have a history of grace and love that rises above the turmoil.

While religious intolerance is not new, the ways in which it spreads have changed. New technologies are being used as tools to spread intolerant views, and those who hold such views seem to be getting bolder than ever. The internet, for example, provides an opportunity

> **"All of us have to fight the rise of anti-Semitism and hateful rhetoric against those who look, love, or pray differently."**[4]
>
> *– Barack Obama, former US president*

for intolerant people to share their views in ways that were impossible in the past. The anonymity that the web provides may encourage people to say things they would not feel comfortable talking about in person. And discussing intolerant views online with like-minded people can reinforce hateful feelings. Such forums can stir up anger that leads to tremendous suffering. Bowers posted the following online just before his attack at the Tree of Life synagogue: "HIAS [Hebrew Immigrant Aid Society] likes to bring invaders in that kill our people. I can't sit by and watch my people get slaughtered. Screw your optics, I'm going in."[5] Bowers posted his message to a website called Gab, a social network which had become popular with right-wing extremists and white supremacists.

The shooting at the Tree of Life synagogue is one of many recent examples of religious intolerance's deadly consequences. In May 2017, Christian militias in the Central African Republic hunted down and killed thirty Muslims. In June 2018, almost 200 Christian villagers were murdered in a killing spree by Muslims in the Plateau State of Nigeria. Six years earlier, another sixty were killed in the same area. On March 15, 2019, a gunman entered two mosques in Christchurch, New Zealand, and opened fire. He left fifty dead and another fifty injured. In April 2019, a terrorist group bombed several churches in Sri Lanka during their Easter services. In the aftermath of the attack, authorities announced that more than 250 Christians had been killed.

Multi-faith spaces encourage people to come together regardless of their faith. This encourages inclusivity by bringing those with differences together into one space.

Many more were injured. Such attacks leave profound scars on survivors, victims' families, and whole communities.

There is a long history of religious intolerance and its terrible effect on humankind. But today, many people are resisting this growing trend. Through education, cooperation, and understanding, activists hope to reduce religious intolerance and violence. They hope this will lead to a more compassionate future for communities around the world.

WHAT IS THE HISTORY OF
RELIGIOUS
INTOLERANCE?

The concept of intolerance has existed as long as humanity itself. Throughout history, people have attacked those whom they have judged as different. Sometimes, the goal is to change those people's views. Other times, the goal is to eliminate those people. This fear-driven mindset—the fear of someone different—has been a factor in human civilizations for thousands of years.

Intolerance is a person or group's unwillingness to permit freedom of expression, including in religious matters. The inability to accept others can be rooted in any number of factors, ranging from gender and ethnicity to clothing and hairstyle. Intolerance based in religion, in particular, has demonstrated a remarkable degree of durability. Religion's important links with culture, morality, and tradition make religious intolerance an especially complex force. Such intolerance is as powerful and destructive today as it was in ancient times.

IN ALL ITS MANY FORMS

Religious intolerance exists in many different forms. One is intolerance between two religions. This is known as interfaith intolerance. An example might be a person of the Islamic faith who is unwilling to

12

Religious intolerance can often be the result of fear or lack of respect for others. Groups sometimes march to bring awareness to a problem.

tolerate anyone with Jewish beliefs. Interfaith intolerance has been the foundation for some of the most horrific conflicts in history.

Another type is called intrafaith intolerance. In this instance, a person of one faith is unable to accept the beliefs of someone within the same faith who follows a different form or denomination of that faith. An example of this would be a Catholic Christian being intolerant of a Protestant Christian. Founding Father Benjamin Franklin made note of this type of religious intolerance when he wrote, "The primitive Christians thought persecution extremely wrong in the Pagans, but

> **"The primitive Christians thought persecution extremely wrong in the Pagans, but practiced it on one another. The first Protestants of the Church of England, blamed persecution in the Roman church, but practiced it against the Puritans."** [6]
>
> *– Benjamin Franklin,*
> *Founding Father*

practiced it on one another. The first Protestants of the Church of England, blamed persecution in the Roman church, but practiced it against the Puritans."[6]

A third form of religious intolerance involves a secular, or nonreligious, group of people refusing to accept those with religious beliefs. An example would be people of a town composed mostly or entirely of nonreligious people refusing to allow a Jewish family to move in for fear that their beliefs would somehow disrupt the harmony of their community.

A fourth form is essentially the reverse of this—a religious group feels the need to attack a secular group for either violating or refusing to embrace their beliefs. For instance, a religious group may attack atheists, who do not believe in any form of religion or deity. In today's world, the number of secular people is rising. These types of conflicts between the religious and the secular may become more frequent.

FROM THE EARLIEST TIMES

The earliest recorded examples of religious intolerance come from ancient Egypt. Sometime in the mid 1300s BCE, King Amenhotep IV took the throne after the death of his father, Amenhotep III. At the time, most Egyptian people worshipped a variety of gods and goddesses. Amenhotep III had primarily been a worshipper of the god Amun. His name, in fact, meant "Amun is satisfied." Regardless, Amenhotep III allowed his people to believe in other gods. They celebrated these beliefs in numerous ways, including the construction of holy temples and the observance of holidays through festivals.

All of that changed with Amenhotep IV. He was a believer only in Aten, the sun god. In fact, Amenhotep IV changed his name to Akhenaten, meaning "the glory of Aten," then restricted all activities relating to other deities. Many of the temples in which these gods and goddesses were worshipped were funded by the Egyptian government. Akhenaten ceased all such payments, forcing the temples to close. He also outlawed all public observances and celebrations. Then he created an official policy that refused to recognize any other form of worship beyond that of Aten.

There is not enough evidence in historical records to know if Egyptian ruler Akhenaten went so far as to punish those who did not submit to his religious beliefs. It is believed that, at the very least, only those who changed their views to align with Akhenaten's were allowed to hold a position in his government. However, archaeologists have also uncovered statues and carvings of other gods in people's homes during this period. These were likely kept hidden and the gods honored in private. This speaks to the near impossibility of changing someone's religious beliefs through intolerant actions. People may alter their own behavior on the outside when faced with threats or violence, but they maintain their convictions in their hearts.

THE BLOODY CRUSADES

Religious intolerance has led to full-scale conflicts resulting in the deaths of thousands or even millions of people. One of the first major examples of this came in the form of a series of holy wars that would become known as the Crusades. The Crusades would have a profound effect on culture in the Middle East and Europe. They also led to centuries of war, death, and destruction.

In 600s and early 700s CE, the religion of Islam experienced a period of tremendous expansion. The prophet Muhammad founded Islam on the Arabian Peninsula. Soon, it spread as far west as modern-day Spain and Morocco, and as far east as Iran and Pakistan. Islam also reached into the areas now called Israel and Palestine. This region lies between the Mediterranean Sea and the Jordan River. It includes sites that are considered the most sacred among three major world religions—Judaism, Christianity, and Islam. Perhaps the most sacred of all is the city of Jerusalem. For Jews, Jerusalem is the place where Abraham went when God directed him to the Promised Land. Abraham is the founder of Judaism. Jerusalem held Judaism's principle temple. For Christians, this region is where Jesus Christ did most of his preaching and where he died and was resurrected. Jesus is a central figure in Christianity, considered the Son of God and the savior of all Christian believers. And for Muslims, a winged creature carried Muhammad from Mecca to Jerusalem. In Jerusalem, Muhammad ascended into heaven, where he and other important religious figures established the daily prayers for believers.

During the first few centuries of Islamic presence in Palestine, there was some degree of tension between Muslims and existing Christian peoples. But for the most part, they learned to coexist. Christians and Muslims could even intermarry.

Then, in 1095, a leader in the Byzantine Empire named Alexius I Comnenus decided to use military force to overtake the Holy Land. His goal was to spread Christianity in the region and wipe out Muhammad's conquest. He asked Pope Urban II for permission and support in his mission. Urban agreed to help and called up thousands

The Crusades led to a lot of hostility between Christians and Muslims. Some of their effects are still felt today.

of people, both trained warriors and ordinary citizens, to act as soldiers. This is when some historical religious military orders were formed, including the famous Knights Templar.

Over the next two centuries, Christians and Muslims fought bloody battles for control of Palestine. Tens of thousands died as a result, and as Christians' strength grew, so did their tendency toward violence. They even began killing Jews, who had maintained a relatively peaceful relationship with Christians up to that point. In 1096, a group of Crusaders slaughtered hundreds of Jews in several towns in Rhineland, an area that is now part of western Germany.

Historians are still grappling with the overall meaning of the Crusades. Historian Mark Damen of the University of Utah, linking the Crusades to modern forms of intolerance, explains,

"Until we decide what drove our ancestors to this mad exploit, how we became the enemy of our brethren in the East, we will find no safe path out of the morass of intolerance and animosity which characterizes Christian-Islamic relations in the modern world.**"** 7

– Mark Damen, historian

There must be something to be learned from all this somehow. What that lesson is, however, has not been determined so far. Until we decide what drove our ancestors to this mad exploit, how we became the enemy of our brethren in the East, we will find no safe path out of the morass of intolerance and animosity which characterizes Christian-Islamic relations in the modern world.[7]

RELIGIOUS INTOLERANCE IN THE EARLY UNITED STATES

The United States has dealt with the challenges of religious intolerance for hundreds of years. Many Europeans took a dangerous voyage to start a new life in the Americas partly because of religious persecution in their homelands. The hope was that religious freedom would be a feature of this new land—but often this was not the case.

For example, the majority of Europeans who came to America were Christians. This promised a degree of harmony. But at times tensions still broke out between denominations. One common conflict was between Catholics and Protestants. The division showed up throughout the early days of the United States. Protestants made laws aimed toward excluding the Catholics. In Massachusetts a set of laws forbade anyone but Christians from holding public office. And even then, Catholics could not hold office until they renounced the authority of the Vatican, their church's leadership.

In 1779, Thomas Jefferson—who at the time was the governor of Virginia—wrote and attempted to pass a bill that recognized the rights of citizens regardless of their religious bearing. Jefferson could not gain enough support to pass it, but the issue was raised again in 1784, when it was supported by another future president, James Madison. Madison laid out fifteen points as to why a free society should allow all individuals the right to observe their religion without fear of punishment. He even went as far as to say that government had no right to interfere in religious matters. His views on church and state became one of the cornerstones to religious freedom in the United States.

THE HOLOCAUST

One of history's deadliest, most sobering examples of religious intolerance leading to violence is the Holocaust. This mass murder of Jews and other groups blended religious intolerance with forms of intolerance based on race, culture, sexuality, and other factors. The Holocaust stemmed from the white supremacist ideology of German dictator Adolf Hitler and his Nazi Party. In 1908, when he was living in Vienna, Austria, long before coming to power, Hitler began to form the notion that Jews were responsible not only for his own misfortunes but for those of Germany as a whole. Anti-Semitism was already widespread in many parts of Europe.

During his time as a soldier in World War I (1914–1918), Hitler decided that Jews were responsible for Germany's ultimate defeat in that conflict. His hatred deepened during the period of profound

The Holocaust during World War II was one of the worst episodes of religious intolerance and violence in history. Jewish people were hunted down and brought to concentration camps or walled off in ghettos.

economic hardship that the nation endured in the war's aftermath. By the time he became involved in formal politics—joining the German Worker's Party in 1919 and then creating the Nazi Party one year later—he had decided that Jewish people were the curse of Europe and needed to be purged. In 1922, he made his intentions clear when he told a journalist, "Once I really am in power, my first and foremost task will be the annihilation of the Jews."[8] His hatred is an example of how religious and racial intolerance can be mixed with political and economic issues.

The atrocities committed during the Holocaust, which Nazi Germany carried out from 1938 to 1945, were broad in scope. Nazis seized Jewish homes, businesses, and other valuable property such as art and jewelry. They burned synagogues to the ground. They beat Jewish citizens in the streets, and police arrested Jews or shot them without cause. The lucky ones sneaked out of the country, where they at least had a chance to start new lives elsewhere. But the unlucky were sent to camps in remote areas, where they were forced to work under appalling conditions, tortured, used for medical experimentation, or killed outright. Approximately 6 million Jews died as a result of Nazi persecution, and it stands as one of the most harrowing examples of religious intolerance in human history.

A CLEAR FOREWARNING

Hitler made his hatred of Jews and their religious beliefs very clear to the German public long before he became the country's leader. He did this in a book called *Mein Kampf*, which means "My Struggle" in German. The book became a nationwide bestseller and contained numerous anti-Semitic rants.

And yet, with these dark feelings made public, Hitler was still allowed to seize power over the German nation. The German people struggled after losing World War I. Their economy was in ruins, and their national pride was wounded. Hitler used this to his advantage by promising to restore the nation to its former glory. And the people, so angered by their misery that they largely overlooked Hitler's stated hatred for Jews, threw their support behind him. Historian Benjamin Carter Hett, in his 2018 book *The Death of Democracy: Hitler's Rise to Power and the Downfall of the Weimar Republic*, wrote, "The Nazis would have been unthinkable without the First World War." By playing on a combination of economic fears and racial prejudices, Hitler and his Nazi Party were able to seize power in the 1930s. Until their final defeat in 1945, they campaigned to murder as many Jews as possible.

Benjamin Carter Hett, The Death of Democracy, *New York: Henry Holt and Company, 2018. p. 232.*

IN THE NEW MILLENNIUM

A modern example of aggression toward others on religious grounds is the events of September 11, 2001, a date commonly referred to as 9/11. Osama bin Laden, leader of the terrorist group al Qaeda, had declared a holy war on the United States in 1998. This included the issuing of a fatwa—a religious decree of the Islamic faith—to kill Americans in large numbers.

Bin Laden's motives for these attacks combined religious and political factors. Among his stated motives was the United States' political support of Israel, a mostly Jewish nation that has experienced a great deal of tension with Muslim communities over the years. There was also the United States' involvement in the Gulf War (1990–1991) against Iraq, a nation with a Muslim majority. In 1998, Bin Laden issued a fatwa specifically concerning the Gulf War, citing the death of thousands of Iraqis and the economic hardship that the United States placed on Iraq in the war's aftermath. Then he stated, "On that basis, and in compliance with Allah's order, we issue the following fatwa to all Muslims: The ruling to kill the Americans and their allies—civilians and military—is an individual duty for every Muslim."[9] Bin Laden's statement is a clear example of how people use political issues in an attempt to justify intolerant behavior.

The 9/11 attacks were Bin Laden's most devastating act. Terrorists working for his organization designed a plan to hijack airliners loaded with fuel and fly them into

"On that basis, and in compliance with Allah's order, we issue the following fatwa to all Muslims: The ruling to kill the Americans and their allies—civilians and military—is an individual duty for every Muslim." [9]

– Osama bin Laden, al Qaeda terrorist leader

civilian and military targets in the United States. On September 11, 2001, four planes were hijacked, three of which hit their targets—two flew into the World Trade Center skyscrapers in New York City, and one crashed into the Pentagon, the headquarters of the Department of Defense, in Washington, DC. The fourth, intended for an unknown target, went down in an open field in Somerset County, Pennsylvania. After learning of the other attacks, the passengers tried to take control of the airplane from the hijackers, and the plane crashed in the ensuing struggle.

Nearly 3,000 people lost their lives in the 9/11 attacks. And Bin Laden, in a letter to the American people issued in November 2002, made it clear that his motives were both political and religious, mostly involving US support of attacks against Muslims at various times and places around the world. Bin Laden also made a point of mentioning his resentment of Jews, calling for aggression by Muslims against both Jews and Christians worldwide. In the letter, he selectively quotes from the Quran, the Islamic holy book, to justify attacks on members of other religions. He goes on to repeat conspiracy theories about Jews controlling the West: "The Jews have taken control of your economy, through which they have then taken control of your media, and now control all aspects of your life making you their servants and achieving their aims at your expense."[10]

As a result of the 9/11 attacks, tensions between Muslims and non-Muslims skyrocketed across the United States and elsewhere. In some cases, these tensions led to acts of violence and paranoia toward Muslims. Many non-Muslim Americans wrongfully associated all Muslims with the actions of Bin Laden and al Qaeda. In Texas, a man angered by the events of 9/11 shot three other men, all of whom he assumed were Muslim. Two were killed and another was

The attacks on September 11, 2001, caused a lot of fear and hostility between Muslims and non-Muslims in the United States. Muslims have faced threats and violence after these terrorist attacks.

left blinded in one eye. The shooter, meanwhile, claimed he felt that members of the US government "hadn't done their job, so he was going to do it for them."[11]

In some cases, people were attacked who were not Muslim but had a supposedly Muslim appearance. One such example was an assault on Dr. Prabhjot Singh, who lives in Manhattan and is of the Sikh faith. Sikh men generally wear a turban—a long length of cloth wound about the head—and have beards. Various styles of turbans and beards may also be associated with Muslim men. But the Sikh religion is not related to Islam. Nevertheless, Singh was mistaken for a Muslim, referred to as both a terrorist and "Osama," and then beaten by a group of young men. He survived the attack and later spoke out about how to eliminate this kind of prejudice: "Ultimately, to simply punish the individuals who've acted out on hate crimes is insufficient. More broadly, we need to have a real national conversation around who looks American, what does it mean to be American."[12]

Much of today's religious intolerance has its roots in the conflicts of the past. Though many of the world's major religions are closely connected, differences in beliefs and doctrines, amplified by cultural, political, and racial intolerance, continue to result in discrimination and violence. A wide variety of examples demonstrate how religious intolerance continues to harm innocent people around the globe.

"Ultimately, to simply punish the individuals who've acted out on hate crimes is insufficient. More broadly, we need to have a real national conversation around who looks American, what does it mean to be American." [12]

– Dr. Prabhjot Singh, victim of a religiously motivated hate crime

HOW IS RELIGIOUS
INTOLERANCE AFFECTING
SOCIETY?

Incidents of religious intolerance have a deep impact on society. A single event like the shooting at the Tree of Life synagogue in Pittsburgh can send ripples throughout the world and leave scars on a community. The impact can last a generation or longer.

The evidence suggests that religious intolerance has recently been on the rise in most countries. "Religious hostilities increased in every major region of the world except the Americas," stated a Pew Research Center report in 2014.[13] This involves not just rival religious groups but also governments attempting to establish state-authorized religions by severely limiting the freedoms of those who worship in a different manner.

The Pew Center published another report in 2016 on this issue, and the findings were alarming. It determined, for example, that 28 percent of all the countries in the world had what it considered "high" to "very high" degrees of restriction on religious worship. That number represented fifty-five out of the 198 nations. It was a notable increase from the 20 percent reported in 2007. The study indicated a steady climb that peaked in 2012 at 29 percent. The numbers dropped slightly in the following two years, then began to rise again. And it is likely they will continue to rise in the future, according to

Andrew Boyd, a spokesman for the organization Release International, who pointed out: "We're seeing an upwards curve, an alarming rise in persecution."[14]

Among the most populous countries in the world, those that had the highest degree of intolerance included Russia, India, China, Egypt, Turkey, and Indonesia. China was at the top in terms of governmental restrictions. And India had the highest level of what Pew called social hostilities, incidents of religious hostility carried out by private citizens rather than by government authority.

The most harassed group worldwide was Christians, with Muslims second and Jews third. There are roughly 2.2 billion Christians and 1.7 billion Muslims out of a global population of 7.6 billion. But the fact that Jews experience the third-highest level of religious intolerance is startling relative to the fact that there are only approximately 13 million people of this faith worldwide—just 0.17 percent of the world population. The Pew Center found that Jews were targeted in eighty-seven of the 198 countries examined during the course of its study, even though Jewish populations in most places are relatively small.

"We're seeing an upwards curve, an alarming rise in persecution."[14]

– Andrew Boyd, Release International

RELIGIOUS INTOLERANCE BEYOND GOVERNMENT INFLUENCE

Intolerant religious groups that operate beyond government influence are becoming more numerous, more determined, and more violent.

THE DEEP AND LASTING EFFECTS OF INTOLERANCE

For the victims of religious intolerance, the psychological trauma can cut deep and linger for a lifetime. While there are support groups and mental-health professionals, victims often have difficulty finding specialized attention for their specific trauma. Specific events create this kind of trauma, but the effects can be kept fresh by societies where religious hatred is faced on a daily basis. Some counseling groups have developed in the United States to address victimization through religious intolerance, but many places do not have this level of support. For many, it may be hard to find any kind of mental health help.

These groups may act in parallel to governmental aims, but they have their own agendas as well. A 2017 study of Christian persecution draws a clear picture of this. In Nigeria, for example, Andrew Boyd noted that "hugely unreported are Fulani militants, Muslim herdsmen, being armed and they are attacking Christian villages in the north of the country and the tactics that they are using appear to be well coordinated and planned."[15] When religiously motivated attacks happen in this region, there is little protection or recourse for the victims.

Other aspects can complicate religious violence as well. Religious beliefs can become entwined in other aspects of cultural identities, such as ethnicity. So even when people are not particularly religious, their pride in their ethnic heritage alone may justify aggressive behavior in their minds. Such aggression can lead to violence if governments are unable to protect their citizens. If a region's governmental authority is weak, intolerant religious authorities may fill the void. "A weak state allows these kinds of groups to be active in the first place," says

Religious, cultural, and ethnic identities can sometimes overlap. Someone who is intolerant of one identity may show intolerance toward an overlapping identity.

German researcher Matthias Basedau, who carried out the study in sub-Saharan Africa. "Their radical ideology becomes more attractive to people if the state does not provide adequate public services and the politicians are corrupt."[16] Then groups take action upon their perceived foes.

Many modern conflicts feature religious extremists, who typically combine extreme beliefs with an unwillingness to consider any other viewpoint. Many extremists then take the matter a step further by considering anyone with a different viewpoint a target. They refuse to recognize the fundamental value of those who believe differently, and as a result place them in a different class—one that is not entitled to the same basic considerations and protections as themselves.

"A weak state allows these kinds of groups to be active in the first place—their radical ideology becomes more attractive to people if the state does not provide adequate public services and the politicians are corrupt.**"** [16]

– German researcher Matthias Basedau

In the study of sub-Saharan Africa, radical Muslims in certain areas were responsible for violence against not just non-Muslims but also against members of their own faith. The Muslim populations of Africa's sub-Saharan region were generally considered moderate and mainstream. But in countries such as Mali, Nigeria, and Somalia, radical Muslims attempted to spread their extreme views to moderate Muslims through intimidation and force.

THE THINKING BEHIND INTOLERANCE

The factors that lead a person to practice religious intolerance are many and varied. There is no standard path to extremism, but there are some elements that appear to be common. A recent trend among extremists relates to age. For example, a study determined that the age of the average extremist Islamist terrorist in Europe between 2001 and 2009 was almost twenty-eight years old. By 2016, however, that figure had dropped to around twenty. One of the conclusions from this statistic is that it previously took many years of programming to radicalize a person, whereas in recent years the decision appears to be more impulsive. In some cases, it is partly a matter of young people wanting to demonstrate rebellious behavior against authority figures. The parents may be more moderate in their beliefs and therefore never consider extreme activities. A young person, therefore, may embrace extremism as a way of creating a rebellious identity.

During the 2010s, the average age of extremists in Europe dropped. Some already had intolerant views or were simply rebellious.

In some instances, a young extremist may have already harbored an active intolerance toward members of other religions, then later embrace extremist beliefs simply as a way of justifying their actions. For example, a young man from a Christian household who isn't particularly religious may develop a hatred for Muslims or Jews. In search of some kind of justification for his actions, he embraces a hateful sect of Christianity. Then, equipped with an additional religious motivation, he acts upon his prejudices.

When traditional sources of stability, such as the government, are viewed as unreliable, corrupt, or ineffective, people may turn to extremism. Faith in something greater can provide a person with fulfillment. An extremist may begin to see violent acts against

THE ROAD TO RELIGIOUS HATRED

The way in which a person develops a sense of religious intolerance so powerful that it leads to hatred can occur so slowly that no one notices. Robert Gregory Bowers, the killer in the Tree of Life synagogue shooting, was said to be a cheerful person who liked cars, beer, and action films. He did own some guns, and he did have a mistrust of the government. But this description also fits millions of other Americans.

An investigation into his life, however, uncovered a disturbing progression. He started to become fascinated with conspiracy theories, in which mysterious people were responsible for famous crimes or running secret governments that controlled the world. Then he began listening to a radio talk show with an ultra-conservative host. The host believed, for example, that the United Nations was not really an organization dedicated to peace, but rather one bent on destroying America. Bowers worked as a volunteer archiving episodes of this program, which thrilled him tremendously. Eventually, however, he drifted away from the show in search of groups that were even more extreme. He found them online. Some of these groups were openly anti-Semitic. Not long after that, he went on a killing spree that left eleven innocent people dead.

nonbelievers as not only sensible but also necessary for the protection of their extremist ideology.

Another powerful motivator behind acts of religious intolerance is the promise of some kind of paradise upon death in reward for carrying out a supposedly holy mission of hatred against members of other faiths. Christianity, Islam, and other faiths have some form of afterlife as part of their belief systems. Extremists may use this afterlife concept to encourage followers to carry out murderous or even suicidal acts of violence against practitioners of other religions.

A person who is already struggling in life may find messages about a holy mission and paradise after death seductive.

On a much larger scale, religious intolerance is often driven by a desire for religious cleansing within a community or society. The goal is to create a society that is supposedly pure. In such a society, all people think the same way and have the same beliefs. The practice of religious cleansing has often been one part of a larger crusade toward ethnic cleansing, where the aim is to return a societal population to some kind of ethnic purity. This represents yet another example of how religious and ethnic prejudices often intertwine.

Examples of this are numerous throughout history. Starting in the 800s BCE, the Assyrian Empire removed millions of people from lands they had conquered, either forcing them to relocate or using them as slave labor. Jews and Muslims were removed from Spain during purges in the late 1400s and the early 1500s. And more recently, hundreds of thousands of Muslims belonging to an ethnic group called the Rohingya were forced out of Burma by the predominately Buddhist nation's military. The displaced people moved into the already impoverished nation of Bangladesh. One refugee told a reporter, "We have left [everything] behind now. Our house and fields have been burned so we can not earn our living there any more. When the military started shooting in our village, we quickly took my children into the jungle and hid them; they were scared from the dangers in the wild. But, when I went back to check on the house, I saw right in front of my eyes, that many people had been killed."[17]

Religious intolerance is also a product of ignorance. While it is true there are clear differences from one religion to another, it is also true that there are some similarities. The refusal to consider these similarities often breeds the kind of hatred that leads to extremist

"When the military started shooting in our village, we quickly took my children into the jungle and hid them; they were scared from the dangers in the wild. But, when I went back to check on the house, I saw right in front of my eyes, that many people had been killed." [17]

– Rohingya refugee

views and actions. When people have already decided that their way is the right way, they may then assume that any other way must be wrong. Related to all this is the natural human fear of being wrong. A religious extremist may refuse to consider the views of another because they know there is the possibility of discovering something that undermines their own beliefs. This particular problem has a way of building upon itself. A person with extremist beliefs may reach a point where they become so invested in their beliefs that altering them becomes virtually impossible.

METHODS OF RELIGIOUS INTOLERANCE

When religiously intolerant governments seek to enforce their beliefs, they are able to create restrictive laws and regulations. Governmental authority gives these regimes the ability to control and punish people.

In recent years, Russia has come under fire on the international front for enacting such laws. In 2016, the Russian government, with President Vladimir Putin's approval, passed a law severely restricting evangelical behavior. This means citizens are not permitted to spread any religious belief outside of a formal house of worship or other recognized religious site. Forbidden behavior includes conducting missionary work, teaching and interpreting scripture, preaching, or any other actions designed to enlighten or persuade. The Russian government justifies its actions through its own definition of religious

Russian president Vladimir Putin has been criticized for many of his actions. Some of this has been over his handling of legislation governing religion.

extremism. For example, in April 2017 it formally gave Jehovah's Witnesses, a Christian denomination, the extremist label. "It effectively means that holding their beliefs and manifesting them is tantamount to a criminal act in Russia," said Lorcan Price, a lawyer in international religious matters. "They risk new levels of persecution by the Russian authorities."[18]

Similarly, India has laws in place that make it all but impossible to legally convert from the state-sponsored religion of Hindu. These laws forbid people not only from converting to another religion but also from attempting to convert anyone else. These laws have been criticized for their intent and for the fact that little to no evidence appears to be required. Punishments for violators include fines of up to a few hundred dollars and prison sentences of up to three years. The laws are relatively rarely enforced. However, they create an environment of fear for many minority religious communities in India. The great majority of Indian citizens—about 80 percent—are Hindu. Another 14 percent are Muslim, just over 2 percent are Christian, and the rest belong to a variety of other faiths.

In some cases, a government will turn to much harsher threats and forms of punishment. China is officially an atheistic country. Its constitution makes room for religious freedom, but there is little religious tolerance in actual practice. If anything, China's 2017 regulations tightened restrictions on religions, claiming that it is attempting to minimize threats from cults and other extremist groups. Muslims and Christians, in particular, have been frequent targets of Chinese authorities. In 2016 alone, according to the US State Department, China "physically abused, detained, arrested, tortured, sentenced to prison, or harassed adherents of both registered and unregistered religious groups." In reaction, a group of more than 116 Chinese church leaders risked angering their government by issuing a statement, saying, "We believe that these unjust actions are an abuse of government power and have led to serious conflicts between political and religious parties in Chinese society. These actions infringe on the human freedoms of religion and conscience and violate the universal rule of law."[19]

Aside from government-sponsored forms of religious intolerance, many actions are carried out by ordinary citizens. Intolerant actions might include verbal taunts, such as calling attention to or making fun of someone's faith-related choice of clothing. For instance, a person may make a derogatory comment about the full-collar shirt of a priest, the burqa of a Muslim woman, or a Jewish man's yarmulke.

Intolerant citizens also commit destruction of property, physical violence, and murder. In some cases, even people in positions of authority are threatened. In 2015, a vigilante Christian group called the Oath Keepers threatened a judge involved in a case with a woman who refused to issue a marriage license to a gay couple. They expected the judge to uphold the woman's position because it protected Christian values, and if he didn't, then "he needs to be put on notice that his behavior is not going to be accepted and we'll be there to stop it and intercede ourselves if we have to."[20]

"We believe that these unjust actions are an abuse of government power and have led to serious conflicts between political and religious parties in Chinese society. These actions infringe on the human freedoms of religion and conscience and violate the universal rule of law." [19]

– Statement by a group of Chinese church leaders in response to laws suppressing religion in China

There are also more subtle approaches, such as denying someone the chance to purchase a home in a certain neighborhood or denying them employment even though they are the best-qualified candidate. The effect these practices have on the everyday lives of ordinary people is tremendous. One Muslim woman, shocked by news reports of crimes driven by Islamophobia, said, "I become more fearful and avoid going to certain places that I feel might be a risk to my safety. And especially within certain times, I would avoid walking within those areas."[21]

The internet has been a particularly useful tool for those practicing religious intolerance. Billions turn to the internet every day to connect with friends, conduct business, follow current events, and find

The internet is a place where people can escalate their intolerance from hateful comments to extremism. Many terrorist organizations communicate and recruit using the internet.

entertainment. But the internet has also afforded hate groups with all sorts of opportunities. It is particularly difficult to curtail online assaults because of the ease with which content can be posted. Religiously based hatred is also particularly harsh on the internet because of the distance between parties and, in some cases, because the anonymity involved makes the attacker even bolder than they would be in person. The internet has also furnished terror groups with a way for members to communicate that can be hard or even impossible to track or trace.

Religious intolerance has a huge effect on society. In its worst form, it has become a rallying cry for mass murder. In 2014, an extremist Islamic organization called the Islamic State of Iraq and the Levant (ISIL) killed or enslaved thousands of Yezidis—a religious minority in the region. This was an attempt to drive them out of their ancestral lands in northern Iraq. The fear from these attacks also terrorizes millions of innocent people. This religiously driven terror takes an emotional toll on society too.

Even in places where genocide is unlikely to ever occur, lives are still disrupted. And many governments have only addressed the problem with assurances that new laws and enforcement agencies to back them up are forthcoming. However, not nearly enough is being done.

CHAPTER THREE

WHAT ARE PEOPLE DOING ABOUT RELIGIOUS INTOLERANCE?

The battle against religious intolerance has carried on for thousands of years. As long as there has been religious discrimination, there have been people willing to stand up to it. Just as there are groups and even national governments that support religious intolerance, there are also organizations that work to provide greater religious freedom. In many countries, legislation forms a legal framework for religious protections. With legislation in place, governments are then able to combat acts of intolerance through law enforcement and the judicial system.

The United States began enacting laws against religious hate crimes in 1968. This initial 1968 statute made it a criminal act to use, or threaten to use, force for the purpose of willfully interfering with any person because of race, color, religion, or national origin. Another law passed that same year, the Civil Rights Act of 1968, made it unlawful for anyone to be denied housing for the same reasons. In 1996, Congress passed the Church Arson Protection Act. This was designed specifically to protect religious locations, as it became a crime to damage religious property or interfere with a person's religious practice. President Bill Clinton, who signed the legislation, made his intentions clear at the time when he said, "We all know when someone burns a house of worship it must mean that the person committing the crime views the people who worship in that house as somehow fundamentally less human. And that is wrong. We know it's wrong, and we know it violates everything that this country was founded upon. We see a spirit today with Republicans and Democrats here that rejects that and says America is better than that."[22]

President Barack Obama supported a further expansion of this type of legislation in 2009 with the Matthew Shepard and James Byrd Jr. Hate Crimes Prevention Act. The act increased the severity of punishments when people carried out violent acts motivated by any one of a number of factors, including religion, race, and sexual orientation. The act also furnishes funds and technical assistance to agencies involved in investigation and enforcement.

Beyond the United States, other nations have begun enacting new laws designed to protect religious freedoms. In June 2013, Taiwan changed its visa policies to permit missionary workers to enter the country and perform religious duties. In the past, this privilege was

> **"We all know when someone burns a house of worship it must mean that the person committing the crime views the people who worship in that house as somehow fundamentally less human. And that is wrong. We know it's wrong, and we know it violates everything that this country was founded upon. We see a spirit today with Republicans and Democrats here that rejects that and says America is better than that." [22]**
>
> *– President Bill Clinton upon signing the Church Arson Protection Act in 1996*

Religiously motivated crimes are considered major crimes. The Federal Bureau of Investigation handles these crimes.

only given to a select few who were almost exclusively Christian. Now, Taiwan is welcoming Muslims and Buddhists as well, with permission to conduct religious work of their choosing. Praising the fact that Taiwan choose to take a very different course on this issue than mainland China, Iowa senator Chuck Grassley said in a speech, "Just look at Taiwan. It has the same Chinese history, language, and culture as mainland China. And yet, on Taiwan, Christians and other religious groups practice freely. No one gives a second thought to whether this is compatible with their history and traditions."[23] And in Vietnam, the government has been helping to construct new houses of worship, including Christian churches and Buddhist temples,

BRINGING NAZIS TO JUSTICE

For many victims of religious intolerance, closure is critical to the healing process. This involves an act or gesture that resolves the cause of their suffering. For example, if someone is murdered, the family of the victim may not have any sense of closure until the murderer is brought to justice. For survivors of the Holocaust, finding closure has been especially challenging. Many Nazis responsible for the genocide successfully got out of Germany and went to other countries. Survivor Simon Wiesenthal sought closure for the events of the Holocaust.

Wiesenthal had been a prisoner at the Janowska concentration camp, but he escaped in October 1943. After the war, he then went to work tracking down as many fugitive Nazis as possible. This would become the focus of the rest of his life because, as he said, "When history looks back, I want people to know the Nazis weren't able to kill millions of people and get away with it." He and his team tracked down hundreds of Holocaust criminals, including some major figures from Hitler's inner circle. Because of Wiesenthal, many Nazis faced life in prison for their war crimes. And in doing so, he brought some degree of closure to thousands who suffered or lost loved ones.

Quoted in "About Simon Wiesenthal," Simon Wiesenthal Center, *n.d. www.wiesenthal.com.*

pagodas, and monasteries. This support has not only come in the form of governmental permission but also free land and grants to aid in building costs.

In other nations, governments have apologized for the religious intolerance of the past. Former Norwegian prime minister Jens Stoltenberg gave a speech in January 2018 formally apologizing to the Jewish community for the expulsion of Jews from the country during World War II. The nation was under Nazi occupation at the time.

"Without relieving the Nazis of their responsibility, it is time to for us to acknowledge that Norwegian policemen and other Norwegians took part in the arrest and deportation of Jews. Today I feel it is fitting for me to express our deepest apologies that this could happen on Norwegian soil," Stoltenberg said. "All over the world we see that individuals and groups are spreading intolerance and fear."[24]

> **"All over the world we see that individuals and groups are spreading intolerance and fear."** [24]
> – Jens Stoltenberg, former Norwegian prime minister

While there is little doubt that new laws, targeted funding, and an acknowledgement of past wrongs go a long way in the fight against religious intolerance, this struggle also requires on-the-ground enforcement activities. In the United States, investigating hate crimes is part of the responsibilities of the Federal Bureau of Investigation (FBI). It has a Civil Rights program that investigates hate crimes. In the past, the FBI was limited in its response to hate crimes. That changed with the Matthew Shepard and James Byrd Jr. Hate Crimes Prevention Act of 2009, which broadened the terms under which "hate crime" is defined. Upon signing it into law, President Barack Obama celebrated the act as a positive step to "help protect our citizens from violence based on what they look like, who they love, how they pray."[25] The FBI places a greater priority on prevention than ever before. In other words, it seeks to stop crimes of intolerance before they are committed. To do so, the bureau relies heavily on input from local law enforcement as well as ordinary people and organized groups within a given community. The FBI also has task forces dedicated to monitoring known hate groups and internet activity, where clues to forthcoming incidents can often be found.

EDUCATIONAL PROGRAMS

Religious intolerance is often learned at a very young age. Hate is not natural, but intolerance is something for which all people have the potential if it is developed and taught. And since children are highly impressionable, it's important for them to be exposed to tolerant attitudes as early as possible. "They hear others, but kids who think in another way are not the enemy," says Aart Wouters, cofounder of the Kaleidoscoop [Kaleidoscope] School in the Netherlands, which places a strong emphasis on religious tolerance. When talking about teaching tolerance, he says, "You don't make it a closed conversation—that it is only like this, or only like that."[26]

More schools are working lessons of tolerance into their curriculum than ever before. Often, these lessons are developed by the school or school district with participation from outside organizations that specialize in anti-hatred programs. The members of the organization conduct an evaluation of the school's environment. They will look for signs of teasing, harassment, and other forms of intolerant targeting to get a sense of the severity of the problem. The findings of the evaluation will then be shared with the school administrators and other staff. This will help them design a custom program that will best address that school's issues. The students will be shown a presentation, then be broken into smaller groups where they can discuss the issues. The entire group will then be brought back together to compare findings and ideas. The groundwork laid by these discussions makes it easier to build an effective program for the school in question.

Schools can incorporate lesson plans that teach students about other religions and cultures. Students put themselves in others' shoes and learn empathy.

Lesson plans examine the religious intolerance problem from a variety of angles. For example, they might involve exploring aspects of religious hate crimes that have already occurred. Students are asked to put themselves in the position of the various people involved in the incident, such as those who committed the act, those who witnessed it, and those who were targeted. By trying to imagine each perspective, students are encouraged to empathize. This helps halt intolerance.

Another plan examines hate crime legislation and its enforcement. With this approach, a student considers which laws and regulations have been the most effective and which have not worked as well. Students can then discuss what improvements might be made to the laws. This lesson can also teach empathy. Students are given a better understanding of the perspectives of people who are the most common victims of intolerance. In turn, many come to understand that such people are not that different from themselves. Students also gain an appreciation for how the law can help or harm groups who are victimized by intolerance.

There is also an increasing trend to include lesson plans that expose students to different religions. This approach helps children embrace the concept of diversity and accept the differences between cultures. A wide variety of different faiths are generally presented in a simple, accessible manner. Students are then encouraged to learn about each religion in greater detail. Teachers sometimes work these lessons into the classroom to coincide with religious games or holidays. At the same time, educators will be aware that the topic of unfamiliar religions can be sensitive, so certain teaching techniques, such as role-playing, may be avoided.

Yet another approach is taking students on field trips to religious locations, such as various houses of worship. During an interview on the subject with PBS, Linda Wertheimer, a veteran journalist in the areas of both education and religion, spoke about the challenges of such a program with the Wellesley Middle School in suburban Boston, Massachusetts:

> *Wellesley does take the sixth graders every year on a field trip to a mosque and a Jewish temple. They bring in guest speakers of all sorts, and there can be some issues with how you do that. You really have to think carefully about who you are inviting and how you're moderating that discussion. Another aspect of what Wellesley does is, they send a letter out to parents letting them know they teach the course and*

THE ELUSIVE LANGUAGE OF HATRED

Many people want to remove intolerant content from the internet. But the process of doing so appears to be much more difficult than anyone imagined. Even in the age of rapidly developing artificial intelligence (AI), experts say it is very challenging to locate and root out such material because of the subtle nature of language. Program developers are struggling to teach AI to separate content that's acceptable from content that isn't. Daniel Kelley, associate director of the Center for Technology and Society at the Anti-Defamation League (ADL), said in a November 2018 article published by the *Boston Globe*, "You need to have a clear definition of hate speech. It's really hard to define, and it's really hard to have the data that can build the models that can be trained to detect this kind of thing."

Many online companies have been forced to hire people to sit and monitor the content of their sites, which requires a tremendous amount of time and energy. But the technology to have a computer perform the same tasks still doesn't exist. Furthermore, even when technological advancements are made, the people posting the hateful material are quick to find ways around them. For example, they will insert random characters in between the letters and words of their messages, making them nearly impossible for AI to detect. Computer experts continue to search for ways to better detect and report hate speech online.

Quoted in Andy Rosen, "Online Hate Is Spreading, and Internet Platforms Can't Stop It," Boston Globe, November 1, 2018. www.bostonglobe.com.

here's why. They're very transparent with parents about what they're doing.[27]

One of the greatest hurdles to solving religious intolerance is when people lack knowledge about religions other than their own. The main fear is that different religions pose some type of threat.

Past generations have struggled with this largely because of a lack of opportunity to discover other religions and talk with people belonging to those faiths. But just as technology has enabled the spread of intolerance, in the right hands it can encourage tolerance. People can talk to members of different faiths from around the world. Even language barriers present less difficulty than they once did, due to the availability of real-time translators.

PUBLIC ACTIVISM

"Local people need to take up religious freedom themselves. They need to own it." [28]

– Tina Ramirez, Hardwired organization

Beyond the institutions of government and education, religious intolerance is being resisted by ordinary people in ordinary communities around the world. This is where the everyday person can make a real difference. As Tina Ramirez, head of the Hardwired organization, said in an interview, "Local people need to take up religious freedom themselves. They need to own it." [28]

While activism can certainly be undertaken on an individual basis, it is usually more effective to join some kind of group effort. To this end, there are numerous nongovernmental organizations (NGOs) that promote an anti-intolerance agenda. The Anti-Defamation League (ADL), for example, is a primarily Jewish-run organization with a focus on combating anti-Semitism. It was founded in 1913 in the United States and now has more than two dozen offices there and three more abroad. Its stated mission declares, "We value respect in our work and workplace, acknowledging the humanity in others—even as we put forth different views." It states a belief in "the power of

The Southern Poverty Law Center tracks the number of hate groups in America. These groups target people based on race, religion, and other protected classes.

inclusion and uniting people from diverse groups—because we are stronger together than when we are apart."[29] ADL activities include immediate response to reported threats and incidents, legal action, lobbying for improved legislation, and anti-bias educational programs for schools and the general public. The ADL also has outreach programs with organizations that represent other religions. Working together demonstrates to the public how people of differing faiths can cooperate to reduce intolerance.

Another organization that deals directly with religious intolerance is the Southern Poverty Law Center (SPLC). Founded in 1971, it has a strong focus on legal advocacy while defending basic civil rights in the United States. While it stands against all forms of hatred—including intolerance based on race and gender—it has increased its efforts toward religious intolerance in recent years. As an example, the SPLC has closely followed the growing trend in hate crimes toward Muslims. According to the center, the number of recognized anti-Muslim organizations in the United States

"We value respect in our work and workplace, acknowledging the humanity in others—even as we put forth different views." [29]

– Anti-Defamation League, Our Values

has gone from five in 2010 to more than 114 in 2017. The SPLC says these hate groups perceive Muslims as a threat to the very core of American democracy. These groups, the SPLC says, believe the goal of Muslims in America is to "subvert the rule of law by imposing on Americans their own Islamic legal system, Shariah law. . . . These groups generally hold that Islam has no values in common with other cultures, is inferior to the West, and is a violent political ideology rather than a religion."[30] A key part of the SPLC's mission is to track and monitor these hateful groups. Like the ADL, the SPLC welcomes participation from ordinary citizens.

Another way in which the average citizen can become engaged in fighting religious intolerance is through a growing variety of public programs designed to educate people and help them understand other religions. These are usually free to attend. Many are held in public locations such as town halls, schools, libraries, and houses of worship. Others can be accessed online. One common type of public programming is a lecture, during which an expert speaks followed by a question and answer session with the audience. Among the most

Interfaith services and programs create a dialogue between people of different faiths. They can help a diverse community grow together.

common topics are a general overview of religious faiths and the nature and thinking behind extremist attitudes and activities. Programs sometimes feature a panel of experts, with a host moderating the discussion. With the subject of religious understanding, a panel may include representatives from various faiths, such as a Christian priest, a Jewish rabbi, and a Muslim imam.

A more visible activity is some kind of public demonstration, such as an interfaith solidarity march. Participants may march on a public street. The march might start at a church and end at a mosque or synagogue. Many marchers carry signs that have positive rather than negative messages, as the organizers want to create a feeling of inclusion rather than exclusion. Participants are encouraged to bring others with them, to increase the size of the march and thereby strengthen its message. And there is usually some kind of program and reception afterward. Since such an activity is a form of peaceful public demonstration, it is protected by the US Constitution. However, marchers may need to get local permits to use public streets for the demonstration.

A third type of public program, which has become increasingly popular, is known generally as an interfaith ambassadorship. Here, a participant agrees to act on behalf of an organization that promotes interfaith dialogue and peaceful relations. The duties of such an ambassador can be varied. These include fund-raising, updating websites, engaging other members as well as the wider public on social media, contributing to newsletters and other promotional publications, and taking part in public outreach programs. Such outreach programs may include visits to schools or houses of worship. Because ambassadors are considered representatives of their organizations, they are also expected to follow a code of conduct at all times. This includes refraining from any type of negative engagement, even if provoked by religiously intolerant people. It also includes listening to others' points of view even if they differ from the ambassadors', and conducting themselves in an honest and respectable manner so as to build trust.

CHANGING THE LAWS

One of the most effective ways to combat religious intolerance is through legislation and regulation. Once these systems are in place, government agencies along with law enforcement can legally act upon those involved in illegal acts of intolerance such as hate crimes. Effective legislation can also prevent such crimes by discouraging those who are considering them.

Support groups can help victims of religiously intolerant acts. There are many ways that people can help these groups.

Ordinary citizens can take part in the push for improved laws by getting involved in the political process. Among the easiest ways to do this is to contact political representatives. Sending emails or letters can be highly effective if enough people participate. Citizens can also sign petitions. A petition is a formal request, usually to someone in a position of power, signed by people who agree with the request. A petition takes on greater power when more people sign it. Petitions used to be submitted on paper, with as many signatures attached at the end as possible. These days, petitioners can get more people involved online, where one might only have to click a single button to indicate their support. The main value of a petition is that it illustrates to political leaders how many people are behind a certain issue.

Concerned members of the public may also become involved with victim support groups. The damage that religious intolerance causes goes beyond the physical. Victims of intolerant acts can suffer lasting mental and emotional problems. They can carry the fear that, since they were targets once, they may be targeted again. They may lose trust in people around them, and they may be frightened of strangers. They may become unwilling agents of intolerance by developing a hatred for their own religious identity or the religion of their attacker. They will likely experience feelings of vulnerability. And the devastating effects of depression commonly develop in the aftermath of an attack. Perhaps most difficult of all is when a victim feels alone in his or her suffering. There are numerous advocacy groups waiting to lend whatever assistance victims need in order to get their lives back on track. This assistance can take many forms, including legal aid, connections to trusted government authorities, and guidelines for treating both physical and emotional issues.

Society has made clear progress in the battle against religious intolerance. People have started paying attention to intolerant acts rather than looking the other way. Concerned citizens have new options at their disposal. Technological breakthroughs such as the internet, with its vast ability to reach people, have enabled millions to show the whole world what is happening. Simply spreading awareness of the problem has been a huge step in working toward solutions.

So much more still needs to be done, however. Religious persecution remains on the rise in some nations, particularly those with leaders who harbor outmoded attitudes such as religious exclusivity. Narrow-mindedness lies at the core of such thinking, and it is still firmly entrenched in some societies. As long as some dig in their heels and hold onto these toxic ideals, those helping the world change must ask, what's next?

WHAT DOES THE FUTURE HOLD FOR RELIGIOUS INTOLERANCE?

It is unlikely that humankind will ever be entirely free of religious intolerance, but there are some hopeful signs that we are continuing to find ways to deal with it. To understand the potential future for religious intolerance, it's important to first understand how religious demographics exist today and how they are projected to change in the future.

Figures published by the *Guardian* newspaper in August 2018 claim that 84 percent of the world's population subscribes to a recognized religion. Further, the majority of this group is generally younger and has more children than those who claim no faith at all. This suggests the world's population will continue to be mostly religious. Figures from the same article stated that the largest religious group is Christians, with about 2.3 billion followers, constituting around 31 percent of the global population. Next largest is Muslims at 1.8 billion, or 24.1 percent of the global population. Third was Hindus at 1.1 billion, or 15.1 percent.

About 1.2 billion people say they have no religion. But this is not to say that they are strictly atheists, or people who reject belief in

The world will continue to be a religiously diverse place. With diversity will come intolerance, but people can take steps to help make the world a better place.

any deity. Some of them may profess to be spiritual but choose not to associate with a specific faith. This group is growing. There are many reasons people make this choice. One is a dislike of the traditions and ceremonies of formalized religions. Some may disagree with established religions when it comes to social issues, such as LGBT rights. People of this mindset may believe that a person's relationship with a higher power should be on a one-to-one basis, without the interference of an organization. Some people believe spirituality, even without religion, provides them with a moral compass. Cognitive

> **"Spirituality for some people seems to mean merely that they believe in ethical values such as caring about other people. But there are many ethical views that operate on rational principles and empathy without invoking spirituality."** [31]
>
> *– Cognitive scientist Dr. Paul Thagard*

scientist Dr. Paul Thagard notes that while this is a reason for some people to have spiritual beliefs, those beliefs aren't necessary to have moral values: "Spirituality for some people seems to mean merely that they believe in ethical values such as caring about other people. But there are many ethical views that operate on rational principles and empathy without invoking spirituality."[31]

The growth of religion will have a powerful effect on the degree of intolerance society will have to endure. For example, the fastest-growing faith in the world is Islam. The number of people who practice Islam should roughly equal the number of practicing Christians by the year 2050. And it is expected to grow by an astounding 70 percent by the year 2060. If these predictions are correct, it means that Christianity will eventually lose its spot as the most-observed religion on the planet. The one place where Christianity will likely see significant gains is in China, despite that country's restrictions on religious freedom. Some statistics suggest that China will have the world's largest Christian population by the year 2030. China has seen growth of its Protestant population alone by an average of 10 percent each year since 1979.

All of this information suggests that religion is not dying out, as some have suggested. It is true that it is receding in some regions. For example, in western Europe, Christianity has been on the decline for many years. In Ireland, the percentage of observant Catholics

CAUTIOUS OPTIMISM

In the field of law, one of the most encouraging developments toward religious tolerance has been the establishment of legal precedents. These are decisions by judges that can be used as examples for other judges' rulings in future cases. And some of the court decisions in the twenty-first century have helped move society toward greater tolerance. A case was heard in 2009 where a Jewish family had been barred from displaying a mezuzah (a small piece of religious text) outside the door of their condominium. The people who sat on the condominium's board of directors argued that there was a rule in place that no one in the condominium complex was allowed to display things outside their doors, regardless of their religion. And the court agreed with this—until the US Department of Justice urged the court to reverse the ruling on the basis that the condo board's rules were in themselves discriminatory. This precedent was set that the Fair Housing Act applied after homes are purchased too. Another case alleged that a family living in a suburb of Chicago was routinely harassed by one of their neighbors because of their Jewish faith. The judge ordered the neighbor to cease harassing them and pay $15,000 in damages for the pain and suffering he caused. A similar case that used the precedent set by the Chicago case helped a Sikh family who was also being harassed by people in their neighborhood.

dropped from 84.2 percent to 78.3 percent between the years 2011 and 2016. And in Scotland, nearly 60 percent now identify themselves as nonreligious. These areas, however, appear to be the exception rather than the rule. And with religious beliefs clearly on the rise elsewhere around the globe, it is more critical than ever for people to learn tolerance toward those who do not share their faith. Indian activist Mahatma Gandhi stated this clearly when he said, "The need of the moment is not one religion, but mutual respect and tolerance of the devotees of the different religions."[32]

Areas in western Europe are becoming less religious. Even with this decline, other areas of the world are increasingly religious.

THE LEGAL QUESTIONS

One of the most pressing issues that will have a direct effect on the fight against religious intolerance has to do with legislation. What laws will protect the principles of religious freedom, and what laws won't do enough? Which ones will go too far? And what about religious issues of a sensitive nature? How will they be legislated so that all sides are satisfied?

For example, in 2017 a Cato Institute conference presented some difficult questions which, sooner or later, will have to be answered. One was, should a Christian baker legally have to bake a cake for a same-sex wedding? Some Christians have struggled with the topic of homosexuality. Another question asked was, would it be acceptable for public schools to ban religious attire, such as a Muslim's head covering? If so, what would be next? Would a Catholic child be forbidden from wearing jewelry bearing a crucifix or a Jewish student banned from wearing a yarmulke?

The Cato Institute article went on to express fears that such legislation could be twisted and used to support other principles. The article draws the sobering conclusion that, "Neither side wants to protect the rights of the others," but also brings up the point that, "religious liberty should never have become a partisan issue in the first place."[33] All of these difficult matters need to be sorted out sooner rather than later.

A NEW GENERATION OF HOPE

There are some strong signs that religious tolerance is already taking root among younger generations. The study "Reasoning About the Scope of Religious Norms: Evidence from Hindu and Muslim Children in India," published in *Child Development* in June 2018, offers some encouraging evidence. The study was conducted in India, which the Pew Research Center considers one of the five countries with the highest degree of religious intolerance among both its government and its population. Rifts between India's varying religious communities are well-documented and still very tense, particularly between Hindus

In India, there has been tension between different faiths. But in some studies, children have shown to be tolerant of others outside of their faith.

and Muslims. And yet, the study found that a surprising percentage of children willingly and independently demonstrated religious tolerance among their peers.

The survey was conducted among sixty-three children, ages nine to fifteen. And the location of the study was Gujarat, a state in northwestern India with a long history of religious violence. With this in mind, the study subjects were chosen in part due to the likelihood that the area's violent past might affect the children's upbringing and, as such, their attitudes toward those of differing beliefs. However, this turned out not to be the case. The children were read vignettes of members of both the Hindu and Islamic faith violating certain aspects of their own religion. They were also read vignettes of children of one faith doing something against the traditions of the other faith.

The children were then asked their opinion of what those violators did. What the researchers discovered was that 67 percent of the children felt that it was wrong for a Hindu to violate a Hindu rule. On the other hand, only 9 percent felt it was wrong for a Muslim to violate a Hindu rule. This indicated the children believed that rules of one religion don't apply to members of another religion. The majority clearly believed that a person should be true to his or her own faith. That same person was not, however, obligated to honor the lessons of a faith beyond his or her own. This in itself was critical to the study because, as authors Mahesh Srinivasan, Elizabeth Kaplan, and Audun Dahl wrote, "conflicts arise when members of one religion apply their norms to members of another religion."[34] That simple idea, the researchers felt, lay at the very core of religious intolerance.

"Conflicts arise when members of one religion apply their norms to members of another religion."[34]

Mahesh Srinivasan, Elizabeth Kaplan, and Audun Dahl, "Reasoning About the Scope of Religious Norms: Evidence from Hindu and Muslim Children in India"

THE IMPORTANCE OF MODERATE VOICES

Religious intolerance is practiced mostly by people who believe their way is the only way. They believe anyone who thinks differently is wrong. One highly public example of this thinking came from the prime minister of Hungary, Viktor Orban, who wrote an editorial in 2015

Many people denounce the violent acts committed by radicals. Public demonstrations for peace can help build trust between members of different faiths.

complaining about the number of Muslims that were coming to his country as immigrants. When asked if he felt these views represented intolerance, he said, "I think we have a right to decide that we do not want a large number of Muslim people in our country." He was then further quoted as saying, "The Islamic religion and culture do not blend with Christian religion and culture; it is a different way of life."[35]

But the majority of people of faith are more moderate in their thinking. A moderate can be defined as someone who not only holds views that are reasonable in nature but also disagrees with the idea of radicalism. People of this mindset practice tolerance regardless of their faith. Even if their views are in direct opposition to someone else's, they do not feel the need to harm the other person or even try to persuade them away from their beliefs. And, it is now thought, they are the best hope for religious tolerance around the world. In other words, the battle for religious tolerance will not be fought between one faith or another. Instead, it will be between those who are radical and the moderates within each faith. And this holds true not just for religious groups but groups of nearly any category, ethnic, economic, political, or otherwise.

One of the criticisms toward moderates in recent years is when they are unwilling to speak out against radical behavior. Moderates are often afraid to oppose extremists of their own faith. In some cases, this is out of fear of being viewed as a traitor and possibly risking some kind of retaliation. Moderates sometimes become the target of scorn and are often ignored as being of little use to their faith. But at the same time, they are often unwilling to speak out against people of other faiths too. They end up in a kind of trap where they feel unable to act on the issue of intolerance.

There have been calls to reverse this trend in recent years. For example, since the 9/11 attacks, the United States has seen numerous attacks on Muslim citizens and those merely perceived to be Muslim. This follows the idea that all Muslims are extremists who support terrorism. This is not the case, of course, as the great majority of Muslims are moderate by nature with no interest in harming anyone. But some people would like to see a united moderate front of Muslims take a stand against extremism.

For example, an article in the *Huffington Post* from 2015 called for a public response by moderate Muslims against recent, deadly

Dialogue and respect are important parts of building an inclusive community. This can lead to new friendships.

activities by extremists. This included the armed attack on the offices of the satirical newspaper *Charlie Hebdo* in Paris, France, which killed twelve people and injured another eleven. In the article, the writer stated, "Modern, moderate Muslims all over the world, particularly those living in secure environments, must speak out more to denounce and further isolate the extremist elements. These moderates have shown courage and solidarity with non-Muslim victims of the depravity of the minority and they can do more, for the sake of the true essence of Islam."[36]

Many experts on the issue of religious intolerance firmly believe that the best way forward is through interfaith cooperation. Moderates are willing to listen, work together, and be understanding. While any set of beliefs can be twisted to suit radical ideas, moderates refuse to take this route. In 2005, moderate Christian and former Missouri senator John C. Danforth wrote in the *New York Times*, "For us, religion should be inclusive, and it should seek to bridge the differences that separate people. We do not exclude from worship those whose opinions differ from ours. Following a Lord who sat at the table with tax collectors and sinners, we welcome to the Lord's table all who would come. Following a Lord who cited love of God and love of neighbor as encompassing all the commandments, we reject a political agenda that displaces that love."[37]

> **"For us, religion should be inclusive, and it should seek to bridge the differences that separate people. We do not exclude from worship those whose opinions differ from ours."** [37]
>
> — *Former Missouri senator and moderate Christian John C. Danforth*

Similarly, and just as encouraging, was a group of Muslim men and women in Washington, DC, who launched what they called the Muslim Reform Movement in December 2015. While holding a press conference, they issued a declaration with a preamble that included the following:

> *We stand for a respectful, merciful and inclusive interpretation of Islam. We are in a battle for the soul of Islam, and an Islamic renewal must defeat the ideology of Islamism, or politicized Islam, which seeks to create Islamic states, as well as an Islamic caliphate. We seek to reclaim the progressive spirit with which Islam was born in the 7th century to fast forward it into the 21st century. We support the Universal Declaration of Human Rights, which was adopted by United Nations member states in 1948.*[38]

Former UN Secretary General Kofi Annan pushed for religious tolerance. His work in advancing human rights earned him the Nobel Peace Prize.

The movement is also built upon the following points: *We reject interpretations of Islam that call for any violence, social injustice and politicized Islam. . . . We invite our fellow Muslims and neighbors to join us. . . . We reject bigotry, oppression, and violence against all people based on any prejudice, including ethnicity, gender, language, belief, religion, sexual orientation and gender expression. We are for secular governance, democracy and liberty. . . . Every individual has the right to publicly express criticism of Islam. Ideas do not have rights. Human beings have rights. . . . We stand for peace, human rights, and secular governance.*[39]

If more people align with these ideals, humanity will begin to move away from religious intolerance and into an age of acceptance. And then, perhaps, everyone can live in a world that reflects the words of former United Nations Secretary General Kofi Annan: "We may have different religions, different languages, different colored skin, but we all belong to one human race. We all share the same basic values."[40]

"We reject interpretations of Islam that call for any violence, social injustice, and politicized Islam. We invite our fellow Muslims and neighbors to join us. We reject bigotry, oppression, and violence against all people based on any prejudice, including ethnicity, gender, language, belief, religion, sexual orientation, and gender expression."[39]

– Declaration of the Muslim Reform Movement, 2015

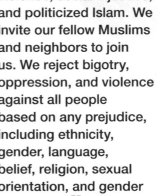
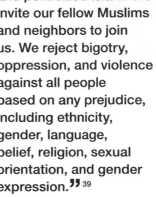

SOURCE NOTES

INTRODUCTION: A MASSACRE IN PITTSBURGH

1. Quoted in Rich Lord, "How Robert Bowers Went from Conservative to White Nationalist," *Pittsburgh Post-Gazette*, November 10, 2018. www.post-gazette.com.

2. Quoted in Lord, "How Robert Bowers Went from Conservative to White Nationalist."

3. Quoted in Nicole Chavez, Emanuella Grinberg, and Eliott C. McLaughlin, "Pittsburgh Synagogue Gunman Said He Wanted All Jews to Die, Criminal Complaint Says," *CNN*, October 31, 2018. www.cnn.com.

4. Quoted in "What We Know About the Shooting at Tree of Life Synagogue in Pittsburgh," *USA Today*, October 27, 2018. www.usatoday.com.

5. Quoted in Campbell Roberts, Christopher Mele, and Sabrina Tavernise, "11 Killed in Synagogue Massacre; Suspect Charged with 29 Counts," *New York Times*, October 27, 2018. www.nytimes.com.

CHAPTER ONE: WHAT IS THE HISTORY OF RELIGIOUS INTOLERANCE?

6. Benjamin Franklin, *The Life and Letters of Benjamin Franklin.* Eau Claire, WI: E. M. Hale and Company, 1940, p. 41.

7. Dr. Mark Damen, "Ancient to Medieval Christianity: Its Birth, the Rise of Islam, and the Crusades," *Brewminate*, February 3, 2017. https://brewminate.com.

8. Quoted in Lorraine Boissoneault, "The First Moments of Hitler's Final Solution," *Smithsonian*, December 12, 2016. www.smithsonianmag.com.

9. Osama bin Laden, "Jihad Against Jews and Christians," *Federation of American Scientists*, February 23, 1998. https://fas.org.

10. Osama bin Laden, "Letter to America," *Bryn Mawr College*, November 24, 2002. www.brynmawr.edu.

11. Quoted in Bill Mears, "Texas Man Executed for Post-9/11 Murder," *CNN*, June 20, 2011. www.cnn.com.

12. Quoted in Rev. Paul Brandeis Raushenbush, "Prabhjot Singh, Sikh Columbia Professor, Attached in Possible Hate Crime," *Huffington Post*, September 22, 2013. www.huffpost.com.

CHAPTER TWO: HOW IS RELIGIOUS INTOLERANCE AFFECTING SOCIETY?

13. "Religious Hostilities Reach Six-Year High," *Pew Research Center*, January 14, 2014. www.pewresearch.org.

14. Quoted in Caleb Parke, "Christian Persecution Set to Rise 'Sharply' in 2019, Group Warns," *Fox News*, January 7, 2019. www.foxnews.com.

15. Quoted in Parke, "Christian Persecution Set to Rise 'Sharply' in 2019, Group Warns."

16. Quoted in Gwendolin Hilse, "Religious Conflicts on the Rise in Africa," *DW*, September 23, 2017. www.dw.com.

17. Quoted in Colin Dwyer, "Apparent 'Ethnic Cleansing' Is Now Unfolding in Myanmar, U.N. Says," *National Public Radio*, September 11, 2017. www.npr.org.

18 . Quoted in Tim Rymel, "When Is a Religion 'Extremist'?" *Huffington Post*, May 11, 2017. www.huffpost.com.

19. Quoted in Wang Jianguo, "116 Chinese Pastors Sign Joint Statement on the New Religious Regulations," *China Partnership*, September 2, 2018. www.chinapartnership.org.

20. Quoted in Rymel, "When Is a Religion 'Extremist'?"

21. Quoted in Rupert Brown, "How Hate Crime Affects a Whole Community," *BBC*, January 12, 2018. www.bbc.com.

CHAPTER THREE: WHAT ARE PEOPLE DOING ABOUT RELIGIOUS INTOLERANCE?

22. William Clinton, "Remarks on the Church Arson Prevention Act of 1996," *Government Publishing Office*, July 10, 1996. www.govinfo.gov.

23. Chuck Grassley, "Grassley Remarks on Religious Freedom in China and Taiwan," *Chuck Grassley: United States Senator for Iowa*, October 9, 2018. www.grassley.senate.gov.

24. Quoted in "Norway Apologizes for Deporting Jews During Holocaust," *BBC*, January 27, 2012. www.bbc.com.

25. Quoted in "Obama Signs Hate Crimes Bill into Law," *CNN*, October 28, 2009. www.cnn.com.

26. Quoted in Hailey Woldt, "A New Model of Teaching Religious Tolerance," *Huffington Post*, October 17, 2012. www.huffpost.com.

27. Quoted in Victoria Pasquantonio, "Q&A: Can Teaching About Religion Reduce Intolerance?" *Public Broadcasting Services*, December 26, 2016. www.pbs.org.

28. Quoted in Doug Bandow, "Combating the Scourge of Religious Persecution: Changing Hearts and Minds in the Middle East," *Forbes*, February 10, 2017. www.forbes.com.

29. "Our Values," *Anti-Defamation League*, n.d. www.adl.org.

30. "Anti-Muslim," *Southern Poverty Law Center*, n.d. www.splcenter.org.

CHAPTER FOUR: WHAT DOES THE FUTURE HOLD FOR RELIGIOUS INTOLERANCE?

31. Paul Thagard, "Spiritual but Not Religious," *Psychology Today*, October 28, 2016. www.psychologytoday.com.

32. Mahatma Gandhi, *Young India*. New York: B. W. Huebsch, 1923, pp. 317–318.

33. "Religious Freedom, from Past to Future," *Cato Institute*, 2017. www.cato.org.

34. Quoted in Annabelle Timsit, "Children in India Might Be the Future of Religious Tolerance," *Quartz*, June 18, 2018. https://qz.com.

35. Quoted in "Global Restrictions on Religion Rise Modestly in 2015, Reversing Downward Trend," *Pew Research Center*, April 11, 2017. www.pewforum.org.

36. José Ramos-Horta, "Charlie Hebdo: Moderate Muslims Must Speak Out," *Huffington Post*, January 8, 2015. www.huffpost.com.

37. John C. Danforth, "Onward, Moderate Christian Soldiers," *New York Times*, June 17, 2005, www.nytimes.com.

38. M. Zuhdi Jasser et al., "Muslim Reform Movement," *Gates Institute*, December 6, 2015. www.gatestoneinstitute.org.

39. Jasser et al., "Muslim Reform Movement."

40. Quoted in Shirley Jones, editor. *Simply Living: The Spirit of the Indigenous People*. Novato, CA: New World Library, 1999. p. xx.

FOR FURTHER RESEARCH

BOOKS

Josh Allen, *Threats to Civil Liberties: Religion*. San Diego, CA: ReferencePoint Press, 2018.

Craig E. Blohm, *Understanding Judaism*. San Diego, CA: ReferencePoint Press, 2019.

Duchess Harris, *Freedom of Religion*. Minneapolis, MN: Abdo Publishing, 2018.

Geoffrey C. Harrison, *Church and State*. Chicago, IL: Norwood House Press, 2014.

John Micklos Jr., *The First Amendment: Freedom of Speech and Religion*. North Mankato, MN: Capstone Press, 2018.

INTERNET SOURCES

Gary Gutting, "How Religion Can Lead to Violence," *New York Times*, August 1, 2016. www.nytimes.com.

Ewelina U. Ochab, "Religious Persecution - The Ever-Growing Threat to Us All," *Forbes*, January 26, 2018. www.forbes.com.

Ashlyn Webb and Will Inboden, "Religious Persecution Is On the Rise. It's Time for Policymakers and Academics to Take Notice," *Foreign Policy*, July 23, 2018. https://foreignpolicy.com.

WEBSITES

American Civil Liberties Union

www.aclu.com

This website includes information on the First Amendment and highlights court cases, press releases, and blogs about religious freedom.

The Religious Freedom Institute

www.religiousfreedominstitute.org

The Religious Freedom Institute is a university-based project to promote religious freedom. It is now a global organization that also helps defend those who suffer persecution for their beliefs.

The Southern Poverty Law Center

www.splcenter.org

The SPLC started as a civil-rights advocacy organization and now fights all forms of hatred, including religious persecution.

INDEX

IMAGE CREDITS

ABOUT THE AUTHOR

Wil Mara is a veteran author with more than 200 books to his credit, both fiction and nonfiction, for children and adults. His work for children includes more than 150 educational titles for the school and library markets. He is the author of the Twisted series and he has also ghostwritten five of the popular Boxcar Children mysteries. His titles have received excellent reviews not only from consumers but also in all respected journals, such as *SLJ*, *Kirkus Reviews*, *Horn Book*, *Children's Literature*, and others. His first novel for adults, 2005's *Wave*, won the New Jersey Notable Book Award. More recently, his thriller *Frame 232* reached the #1 spot in its category on Amazon, won the Lime Award for Excellence in Fiction, and was a finalist for the Christy Award. He is also an associate member of the NJASL, and an executive member of the Board of Directors for the New Jersey Center for the Book.